A YOUNG SOFTBALL PLAYER'S GUIDE TO

# HITTING, BUNTING, AND BASERUNNING

## ALSO BY DON OSTER

*A Guide for Young Batters & Baserunners*
with Bill McMillan

*A Guide for Young Pitchers*
with Bill McMillan

*A Guide for Young Softball Pitchers*
with Jacque Hunter

*A Young Baseball Player's Guide to Fielding and Defense*
with Bill McMillan

All from The Lyons Press

# A YOUNG SOFTBALL PLAYER'S GUIDE TO
# HITTING, BUNTING, AND BASERUNNING

**Don Oster and Jacque Hunter**

THE LYONS PRESS
GUILFORD, CONNECTICUT
An imprint of The Globe Pequot Press

To buy books in quantity for corporate use or incentives, call **(800) 962–0973, ext. 4551,** or e-mail **premiums@GlobePequot.com.**

The Lyons Press is an imprint of The Globe Pequot Press.

10 9 8 7 6 5 4 3 2 1

Printed in the United States of America

ISBN-13: 978-1-59228-850-2
ISBN-10: 1-59228-850-2

Library of Congress Cataloging-in-Publication Data

Oster, Don.
    A young softball player's guide to hitting, bunting, and baserunning / Don Oster and Jacque Hunter.
        p. cm. — (A young player's guide series)
    ISBN 1-59228-850-2
    1. Softball. I. Hunter, Jacque. II. Title. III. Series.

    GV881.O88 2006
    796.357'8—dc22

                                                                        2005028489

# CONTENTS

# ACKNOWLEDGMENTS

Thanks to all of my present and former players and their parents without whose contributions and hard work this book would not be possible. Special thanks also to present and former assistant coaches Don Sisloff and Dennis Richardson for their help through more than twenty seasons. Robert Holmes, former superintendent of the New Albany-Floyd County Indiana Consolidated School Corporation, had far-reaching vision in promoting athletics for young women. He would be extremely proud of the extent of today's programs.

And finally, thanks to the New Albany, Indiana, High School Athletic Department and Don Unruh, athletic director, for the use of the field where the photos were taken. I also must recognize Diane Carter for her assistance on this book and Brianne Casper and Katy Walton for their help in the photo process.

—*Jacque Hunter*

# INTRODUCTION

Batters have fun. They have fun in games and even practicing is fun. Making good, solid contact and seeing a line drive shoot into the outfield is one of the best feelings a batter can have at any level of play. Hitting and making solid contact with a pitched ball is not easy because both objects are round. Batters and weather forecasters are about the only people who can claim success when they only get it right three or four times out of ten tries. However, to be a good hitter takes several things: a good, positive attitude; use of sound fundamentals; and lots of practice.

We start the book with the profile of a good hitter and then describe several key attributes of the batter and her approach to her turn at bat. With work, practice, and study, in time this description will fit you when you take your place in the batter's box.

The first part of this book is about hitting. Because your softball career is just beginning, it is important that you learn sound fundamentals from the start. In chapter 2 we will teach you basic batting fundamentals that will serve you throughout your career. It starts with bat selection, the grip, setting up to hit, the swing, and follow-through. Making contact is what hitting is all about. When you're making good contact with the ball, the base hits will fall.

Fast-pitch softball is generally pitcher dominated. The batter has a very short time to react and hit the ball following the release of a pitch. In chapter 3 we examine the reaction time based on pitch speed, and you will rapidly understand why a quick bat is necessary for success as a hitter.

The following chapter includes several batting drills to reinforce your use of basic batting fundamentals. These drills also help you develop good hand-eye coordination and a quick, compact swing. Preparing to bat includes more than picking up a bat and walking to the batter's box. In chapter 5, "Getting Ready to Bat," you will learn some things you can do to be prepared to give your best effort each time you step into the batter's box. These include sizing up the other team's pitcher and knowing the game situation and your special job when there are runners on base. Next, in "Making Your At Bat Count," are tips on how to work a pitcher and adjust according to the ball and strike count to get the most out of each time at the plate.

But softball is a team game and hitting isn't all there is to a strong offense and winning games. You need to learn other skills before you can become a complete offensive player, and these are covered in the next chapters. First, team success isn't all about base hits, so every player must know how to bunt. Sometimes a simple little bunt dribbling down a baseline can be a game breaker. In chapter 7, "Bunting Fundamentals," we teach you how to execute sacrifice bunts and bunts for a base hit. A special part of the chapter on bunting also covers the slap hitting technique.

To win, your team must score runs. You won't get a hit every time at bat, but you make a contribution to the team when you advance base runners. In chapter 8 we cover ways you can help your team offense by moving runners into scoring position. Good baserunning can win ball games, and bad baserunning can make it harder to win. If you are blessed with blinding foot speed, you could be a real offensive weapon. However, even the slowest runners should be smart base runners, and smart baserunning is what chapter 9 is about. Most baserunning moves will be directed by coaches, but you also have responsibilities when you're on base. These include knowing the game situation, paying attention to what happens, and knowing how to react.

In chapter 10 we talk about the mental aspects of hitting. Maintaining a positive, aggressive, disciplined approach to each at bat leads to success. Chapter 11 sums up individual and team aspects of the game. You need to understand strategies for advancing runners and the characteristics of a good team offense.

The twelfth chapter, "Common Batter Problems," describes habits batters fall into that can limit their success. Most of the problems with mechanics can be solved by going back to the basic fundamentals and practice drills. Other problems, described as "problems between the ears" have to do with a batter's attitude toward hitting. These are also discussed.

We hope you learn from this book and enjoy reading it. You have arrived at a golden time full of opportunities that didn't exist a decade ago for female athletes, which is discussed in the final chapter. You're getting started on a successful career, remember to have fun all along the way.

**A YOUNG SOFTBALL PLAYER'S GUIDE TO**

# HITTING, BUNTING, AND BASERUNNING

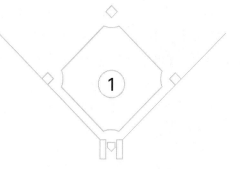

# PROFILE OF A GOOD HITTER

It's the start of an inning. One teammate is at bat, another is on deck, and the good hitter is in the dugout. She is standing at the dugout fence, peering intently at the opposing pitcher. As she studies the pitcher's delivery and speed, she also watches for any variations in the pitcher's motion that may give away a pitch such as a changeup or off-speed pitch. She asks any teammates who have faced the pitcher how fast the pitcher throws and if they saw any breaking pitches.

The teammate who was batting has reached first base, and now our batter is on deck. In the on-deck circle the batter loosely swings a weighted bat to warm up her arms, wrists, and shoulders. The swings aren't hard, just fast enough to get loose. As she swings, she studies the pitcher once again. She notes the pitcher's speed on her fastball and what part of the strike zone she works to with most of the pitches. Almost all of the pitches are fastballs. She knows she can hit this pitcher's best fastball and can adjust to a change of speed or breaking pitch if necessary.

The previous batter has made an out, so it is time to go to the plate. Before leaving the on-deck circle, the batter picks up her regular bat and swings it a couple of times. Her swing is quick, tight, and compact. She knows the game situation: there is a runner on base with one out. As she nears the plate, she looks at the third base coach for a sign. In this game situation, the coach may signal for a bunt to advance the runner, a hit-and-run, a fake bunt, a steal to the runner, or simply to hit away. If the signal is for a steal, she will swing to try to distract the catcher and help protect the runner. Giving up a first strike to the pitcher doesn't bother her at all, she knows she can hit. This batter is prepared to do anything the coach wants—she is a team player with confidence in her ability to execute any option.

As she steps into the batter's box, she peeks at the positions of the infielders at first and third. If either one is playing back, that might be a good place to dump a bunt for a base hit. Or if the coach signals for a sacrifice bunt, she may bunt the ball where the infielder is back and beat the throw to first. If the signal is to hit away, she knows the strike zone and believes she can make good contact with any pitch in the zone. This is a confident batter who has her head in the game.

As she takes her position in the batter's box, her feet are a little more than shoulder width apart, and she is bent slightly at the waist and knees. She is on the balls of her feet and balanced, but with slightly more weight on her back leg. She takes a half swing to make sure she can reach a pitch over the outside part of the plate. Her head is steady, and both eyes are focused on the spot where the pitcher will release the ball. As she takes her stance, she is relaxed but ready.

The batter knows stress and tension can be her enemy. Regardless of how critical the game situation may be, she won't let stress or nervousness interfere with her performance as a hitter. If she starts to feel tense, she will ask the umpire to call a time-out, step out of the box, and take a couple of deep breaths to calm herself. This batter has good self-control.

This player knows that the strike zone is like a rectangle over home plate. It is as wide as the plate, the top is at her armpits, and the bottom is at her knees. She will not help the pitcher by chasing pitches outside the strike zone. From her game experience, practice, and drills, the batter believes she can make good contact with almost any pitch in the strike zone. She can pull inside pitches down the baseline, hit outside pitches to the opposite field, and seldom takes a called third strike. When she is behind in the count, she will go after pitches that are "too close to take." This batter is both confident and smart.

If the coach doesn't signal for a sacrifice bunt with a runner on base, the batter's main objective is to reach base safely and advance the runner. She may hit safely to get on base, but she knows that will happen only three or four times in each ten at bats. The batter will work the count, taking pitches out of the strike zone while being ready to drive any good pitch somewhere into the field. If she makes contact and her effort doesn't result in getting on base, she has a chance of advancing the runner. If the pitcher doesn't give her a pitch to hit, she will take a walk. It's a team game after all, and base runners have a chance to score. This is an aggressive yet controlled batter who will make a contribution to team success.

The batter knows she has a fairly high batting average, but that isn't her main objective. She practices and works hard on batting fundamentals. Picking good pitches and making good contact with the bat are her prime goals. She knows that putting the ball into play puts pressure on the other team's defense because it forces them to make a play. If she consistently makes good contact, the hits will come and the batting average will be okay. This player is a good hitter.

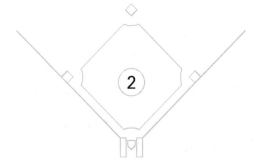

# BATTING FUNDAMENTALS

Timing is the most important element of successful hitting. The movements necessary to get all of the body parts synchronized to make a good swing to contact a ball are called batting mechanics. Good hitters have solid, consistent mechanics that are developed by hours of practice. They develop a muscle memory from repetition in practice until good swings are almost automatic. Making solid contact with a pitched ball is not an easy thing to do for most players. Very few players are blessed with the pure natural ability to be a good hitter.

Most good hitters have worked hard to develop and maintain sound fundamentals throughout their careers. Many elements are involved in the coordination of body parts to make a good swing. This chapter will teach you batting fundamentals.

## GETTING STARTED RIGHT—BAT SELECTION

Many young hitters struggle from the start because they don't have the proper bat. Be involved in selecting your bat. Using sound batting mechanics, you want to develop a quick, compact swing that generates good bat speed. But if your bat is too heavy for your size and strength, your bat speed will suffer. You will probably struggle to make a good swing until you grow up to the bat. To test a bat for proper weight, take the bat handle in your right hand and hold it out at shoulder height. If you can't hold it for thirty seconds, it is too heavy.

Next, hold the bat in both hands. Grip the handle in the joints of your fingers just tightly enough to feel you can control the bat when you swing. Some bats have thick handles, others are thin. (Young players with small hands may need to grip the bat in their palms.) The handle size is mostly a matter of personal preference and feel. Swing bats with different size handles

Grip

that have passed the weight test. The best one is the one that feels good in your hands. Next, take a few easy swings. The bat should feel comfortable in your hands as you swing. As you swing harder, the best bat for you will still feel comfortable and under your control. Don't be concerned about the barrel size of the bat you choose because today's modern bats have an ample surface to make contact with the ball.

**SWING MECHANICS**

The following photo sequence shows a batter with good mechanics. In the following sections we describe each element of the swing.

Stance

Stride

Swing

Contact

Follow-through

### *The Stance—Feet and Body Position*

The stance forms the firm foundation of the body position necessary for a good swing and ball contact. Set your feet a little more than shoulder width apart so that a line drawn across your toes would point toward the pitcher. Your front shoulder should be pointed toward the pitcher. Bend slightly at the knees and waist. You should be balanced slightly on the balls of your feet with slightly more (about 60 percent) of your weight on your back foot.

The directions above have you in a straightaway stance. Some batters set up with their front foot forward, which is called a closed stance. Others have an open stance where the back foot is closer to the plate than the front foot. In the straight stance you are set up to simply stride toward the pitcher (explained below). A batter striding toward the pitcher out of either an open or closed stance has wasted motion, which can adversely affect her balance.

Batting stance

### The Stance—Hands and Head Position

To position your hands to make a good, compact swing with little wasted motion, place your hands level with your back armpit. Your bat should be at a forty-five

Stride

degree angle to the ground. This is a set position to go quickly from ready to contact when you initiate the swing. Batters holding the bat straight up or level to the ground or with their hands too high or too low cannot get their bat into an effective position to swing without making adjustments.

Your head must face the pitcher and be absolutely steady throughout the hitting motion. Any head movement makes it almost impossible to make solid contact with the ball. Both eyes must be focused on the pitcher to pick up the pitch when it is released.

Your eyes must follow the ball all the way to the bat, and you should see the bat and ball make contact. In your stance, you are ready to initiate and make a swing. In the stance position you should be comfortable, relaxed, and ready.

### The Stride

The stride is the first motion preceding initiation of the swing. The swing is a continuous motion from the stride through the follow-through. As the pitcher is in her motion, take a short stride (about two inches) with your front foot toward the pitcher. This starts a forward weight shift. In your stance you had about 60 percent of your weight on your back foot. After the stride you should be balanced, with half of your weight on each foot. During the stride, your head stays still, and your hands remain at the armpit level.

### The Swing

The swing is initiated immediately following the stride. Moving the hands from the ready (armpit level) position in the stance to about the middle of your chest starts the swing. In this position, the knob of the bat is pointed toward the pitcher; the barrel is pointed toward the umpire's position.

Initiate Swing

### *Contact Position*

The next move is to attack the ball by snapping the bat into a contact position with the hands and arms. A weight shift from the balanced position toward the front foot occurs as you swing. Your front hip opens up as you pivot your hips with the swing. At the contact point, you shift to putting 60 percent of your weight on your front foot. Your head should be held steady with your eyes focused on the ball, and your stomach will be facing the pitcher. The toes of your front foot will still be pointed at the plate, and you will pivot up on the toes of your back foot.

Contact position

This is the basic power position of your swing. The movements are synchronized so that you have the combination of hip turn, weight shift, shoulder turn, and bat speed to transfer power to the ball when you make contact. Making contact is a result of keeping the head still, good balance, and hand-eye coordination.

### The Follow-Through

A good full follow-through with the hands, arms, and barrel of the bat indicates that you have hit through the ball, not at it. When the follow-through is finished, you will be facing the pitcher with fully 60 percent of your

Follow-through

weight on your front foot. Your hands and arms will have fully completed the swing.

## POSITION AT THE PLATE

Each person is built differently in terms of height and the length of their arms and legs. However there are some absolutes relating to the position at the plate where you should take your stance. First, you should set up where you will contact the ball slightly in front of the plate, and you should be able to reach a pitch on the outside part of the plate.

Players with short arms may need to crowd close to the plate to reach the outside pitches, which brings up another point. If you must crowd the plate, you will occasionally have pitches thrown very close to your body. After all, pitchers don't have perfect control, and the odds of getting hit by a pitch increase as you crowd the plate. When a pitch looks like it will hit you, roll away from the ball by turning your upper body toward the catcher and dropping your head. This move is to try to protect your head and upper body. If the pitch hits you, it will normally be a glancing blow and hopefully won't hurt as much as a solid hit. It is a good idea to practice this move with a friend using soft rubber balls or tennis balls.

Inside pitch—turn away

## SOME BATTING ABSOLUTES

The following tips will make you a better hitter.

- No matter how successful you may be at the moment, never stop practicing and trying to learn. Remember, even if you're batting .400, you're getting a hit less than half of the time.
- Relax. Muscle tightness brought on by being nervous or stressed will make it difficult for you to make your usual quick, powerful swing.
- Learn the strike zone. When you chase bad pitches, only the pitcher benefits.
- Stay smooth and powerful with your swing. Lunging or overswinging will mess up your mechanics.
- Keep your head steady through the entire swing.
- Hit through the ball to drive it somewhere, then follow through.
- Be aggressive at the plate. Always be ready to drive a good pitch somewhere. Don't look for walks, let them come only when you haven't had a pitch to hit.

◆ Focus your eyes on the ball. Look for it when the pitcher releases the pitch and watch the bat hit the ball when you make contact.

◆ Keep to the fundamentals and maintain a good, compact swing, which is the ticket to hitting a lot of hard line drives.

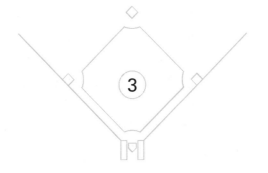

# FAST PITCH—FAST BAT

According to an old baseball saying, good pitching will beat good hitting anytime. This applies as well to fast-pitch softball, and in fact maybe even more so. A good fast-pitch pitcher can basically dominate a game as much or maybe more than a good baseball pitcher. If you doubt this, look back at the run differential of the U.S. Olympic softball team's gold medal performance in the 2004 games. The U.S. team had excellent pitching, which buried the best teams in the rest of the world. The simplest reason for domination relates primarily to speed and distance. From the earliest league play through high school, the fast-pitch pitcher's plate is only forty feet from home plate. A pitcher who can really fire the ball can blow it past any batter who is indecisive about swinging or who has a slow swing.

Now we will examine the allowed reaction time at different speeds for a batter to make a decision about a pitch, then swing to make contact before the pitch is in the catcher's glove: A thirty-mile-per-hour pitch allows the batter about nine-tenths of a second to react and hit the ball. In the earliest years of league play, during the preteen years, this is about the speed of the better pitchers. In the ten- to twelve-year-old age group, a batter with a big, loopy swing may get by fairly well. In this age group the pitchers are usually struggling to throw strikes, and batters usually get some really fat pitches to hit. This batter may even hit some home runs and seem to be on her way to future stardom.

However, as a player advances to the higher age groups, the pitchers improve dramatically. They catch up to and basically surpass the average batter's skills. If a pitch is forty miles per hour, the reaction time for the batter is about two-thirds of a second. The fifty-mile-per-hour fastball allows very little over a half second. At this pitch speed, the batter with the big, loopy, swing-from-the-heels mechanics will be a candidate for a lot of disappointing strikeouts.

These reaction times are the main reason for the previous chapter on batting fundamentals and the drills in the following chapter that teach you how to develop a quick, compact swing. Starting out with the correct mechanics will serve you well in the early years as a batter. In the first years of league play you won't likely face a lot of really good pitchers, so this is a good time to learn the discipline to hit only good pitches. Chasing after bad pitches only helps the pitcher. With your quick, compact swing, you can almost study these slower pitches as they come toward you and still have time to drive a good pitch into the field.

Continue to practice your good batting mechanics as you grow bigger and stronger. When you advance to the higher levels, you will be ready and well equipped to face the faster pitchers. As an example, a pitcher in her early to mid-teens (high school age) can certainly throw pitches at nearly fifty miles per hour. And the good high-school-age pitchers can muster this speed with very good control. Against weaker pitching, the younger league batter may be able to attain a batting average of .600 or maybe higher. When the competition tightens at the older levels, an average between .300 and .400 is very, very good.

Notice here we haven't talked at all about change-ups or breaking pitches. A good advanced softball pitcher may be able to throw breaking pitches that curve in any one of four directions. These are drops, curves, and pitches that rise. A changeup may also curve, but its speed will be slower than a normal pitch. As the pitchers grow and improve, they will add these breaking pitches to their assortment. However, at even the higher speeds the straight fastball will continue to be their best pitch. But when they do throw a breaking pitch or off-speed changeup, the bat speed generated by your solid, compact swing will allow you to make contact most of the time, even if the pitch has you fooled. As stated before, develop good batting mechanics and they will be a major element of your success at any level of play.

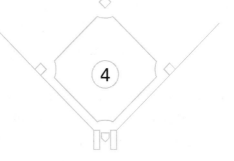

# HITTING DRILLS

The drills in this chapter will reinforce the batting fundamentals you learned in chapter 2. You will be employing the fundamentals in each drill from the stance to the follow-through. Using them, you will develop muscle memory that helps keep your mechanics consistent with each swing. The drills will also improve your hand-eye coordination, helping you to become a better contact hitter. Always remember when going through these drills to set up each time exactly as you would for a turn at the plate in a game.

Becoming a good hitter takes practice, lots of it. At the highest levels of the game, batters continue to work on their mechanics. Very few hitters are so gifted that they can pick up a bat and hit well without practice. Most good hitters work hard to try to perfect their skills. Now that you have learned the batting fundamentals, you must decide how hard you're willing to work to become a good hitter. It all boils down to how badly you want to succeed as a player. Actually some of these drills are sort of fun to do. You can work on several of them by yourself, but others will require another person.

Make sure you practice the drills in a safe place. Using Wiffle balls, soft rubber balls, or tennis balls in these drills may be best because they are a smaller target to hit than a regulation softball. If you are using hardballs, each participant in the drill must always wear a helmet.

## THE TEE DRILL

The tee isn't just for the little kids. Actually you should use a tee for practice throughout your career because one of the benefits of the tee is that you can practice by yourself. All you need is your bat, some balls, the tee, and a backstop to hit into. Buy a tee; it's an important part of your development as a hitter. Again, if you are using hardballs, wear a helmet.

Hitting a ball is a fast, continuous movement, which can be broken down into three major parts to make it easier for you to practice specific body movements when you swing. The first move is the setup and stance, the second is a swing to contact, and the third is the follow-through.

### Setup and Stance

Place a ball on the tee. Set up in your stance with the upright part of the tee in front of your front foot. The toes of both feet should be pointed toward the plate part of the tee. Place your feet a little wider apart than

Stance

your shoulders and bend slightly at the knees and waist. Your weight should be on the balls of your feet with about 60 percent of your weight on your back leg. Relax your hands, arms, and body. Hold your bat level with your armpit and angle it at forty-five degrees to the ground. Your back elbow should be down but not touching your body. Maintain good balance, keep your head still, and focus your eyes on the back of the ball.

### Swing to Contact

Now you are preparing to take a swing. Take a short stride (about two inches) with your front foot. Stay

Stride

balanced, with your weight even on each foot. Start the swing by moving your hands toward the pitcher. When your hands reach the middle of your chest, the knob of the bat should be pointed at the pitcher. The barrel of the bat will be pointed at the spot where the umpire stands.

Next, snap the barrel of the bat to the contact position, stopping it just before it hits the ball. As you move to the contact position turn your hips forward, and roll up onto the toe of your back foot. Your belly will be facing the pitcher. More than half of your weight will be on your front foot, and the toes of the front foot will remain

Contact

Follow-through

pointing at the plate. Your head should be down, with your eyes focused on the ball.

Go through these steps several times without completing the swing to get the feel of the movements. Take care to set up and get into your stance in the same way each time. Make sure you can maintain good balance as you take these steps. Keep your head still and focus on the ball. You will not hit consistently if you are off balance or move either your eyes or head.

### Complete the Swing

After you have gone to the contact position several times and stopped, go ahead and complete the swing by contacting the ball. Do not hit at the ball, but drive through it with your swing. Following contact, let your wrists roll and allow the bat to complete the swing to the full follow-through position. Your head should still be down, with your eyes focused on where the ball was. Your balance should be good throughout the swing and follow-through.

You cannot overpractice the tee drill. All of the elements of good batting mechanics are in this step-by-step process with one exception. The fence drill, which will help you tighten your swing, comes next.

## THE FENCE DRILL

Good hitters have a tight, compact swing. A batter with a big, wide, loopy swing may occasionally make contact and hit a long ball. But this batter will not make consistent contact and will often strike out.

For the fence drill you can use any fence at the ball park or a wall that you can't damage, such as a concrete basement wall. However, in this drill we will refer to a fence.

Stand facing the fence. Place the knob end of your bat against your stomach and step forward until the barrel of the bat touches the fence. Set up and take your batting stance. Take a small stride and go slowly through your swing from stance to the contact point. If you are

Measure

Stride

Contact

moving to the contact position properly, your bat won't touch the fence. Continue to repeat the movement slowly from your stance to contact several times. Increase the speed of the swing and complete it. Continue taking full swings through the follow-through. Your bat may barely tick the fence on occasion, but your swing will be tight.

## MOVING BALL DRILLS

Now that you have learned the fundamentals and have drills to dry practice your mechanics, we will now move on to drills where you make contact with a moving ball.

Concentrate on hitting the back of the ball in these drills. Keep your head steady and watch the bat meet the ball. If you have difficulty making solid contact in the following drills, go back to study the basic mechanics and practice them using the tee and fence drills.

### Soft Toss

This is a common pregame drill you see players using. For soft toss you need two people, some balls, your bat, and a fence to hit into. The tosser kneels on one knee facing the batter, three or four bat lengths from the batter. The tosser should be about one step ahead of the batter's front foot. The batter sets up in her stance. The tosser says "trigger" then tosses a soft lob toward the batter's

Soft Toss

SoftToss

front hip. The batter strides, swings, and drives the ball into the fence. Soft toss is a good practice drill to do with a friend anywhere you have a solid barrier to hit into.

### Playing Pepper

This is an old baseball drill that you can make into a competition. Several players face the batter from a distance of fifteen or twenty feet. The batter should choke up on the bat and make contact but not with a full hard swing. One of the fielders softly tosses the ball underhand into the batter's strike zone, and the batter taps the ball toward the fielders. This drill provides an opportunity to practice timing and bat control. Try to hit each toss to a specific fielder. When you can do this, next try to hit down the line to each fielder in turn. The batter gives up her place at bat and becomes a fielder when she fouls off or misses two or three pitches. This is a nice team drill because of the simultaneous fielding and batting practice.

### The Hitting Stick

The stick used in this drill is usually made of plastic or fiberglass, with a handle on one end and a ball on the other end. Two people participate in this drill, a holder and a hitter. The hitter sets up in her batting stance, ready to stride and swing. The holder with the stick faces the batter at a distance that will allow the ball on the end of the stick to be moved through the batter's strike zone. As the holder says "trigger," the holder moves the ball through the strike zone, and the batter

Swing Stick

strides and hits the ball on the end of the stick. This is a good drill because a batter can get a lot of swings and no one needs to retrieve the ball. Another benefit of this drill is that the holder can deliver the ball to any

Contact

Follow-through

place in the strike zone, and by doing this the batter can practice making contact with pitches in all parts of the zone. Keep your mechanics smooth, a still head, and a tight swing as you hit all of the offerings.

### Pitching Machine

A pitching machine and batting cage setup is a good place to work on swing mechanics and timing. It is particularly good in the early season because a player can get a lot of cuts and contact with moving pitches in a short time. However, no setup is perfect, and the machine batting practice has a few drawbacks. The timing part is okay in that the person feeding the machine shows the ball to the batter before putting it in. This sort of serves as the "trigger" call as in other drills. However, a properly adjusted pitching machine will drill a good pitch on almost every throw. The batter can groove the swing to hit an almost perfect pitch every time, which cheats batters out of learning to lay off bad pitches.

The second drawback is the constant speed. The machine is set at a given speed and once batters see a few pitches, they can time the machine's constant throwing speed and rip each pitch. Batters on the machine don't get the experience of adjusting to the speed differences of real pitchers. We're not necessarily talking about bona fide changeups here, just the slight speed differences naturally occurring from pitch to pitch. Hitting on a machine certainly has a place in training hitters, but it isn't the end-all some coaches think.

### Live Batting Practice

This could be part of a regular team practice, occurring in a cage or on the playing field. It provides a chance for pitchers to practice throwing to batters and for batters to practice hitting. The batting practice pitcher can't always throw at a constant speed, which forces the batters to adjust to the different speeds to make good contact. In live batting practice a batter can learn to lay off bad pitches and look for the good pitch to hit. If a coach or player calls balls and strikes during live batting practice, players can get a good concept of the strike zone, and knowing the strike zone is an attribute of all good hitters. Batters can also get a feel of the pitches that are "too close to take" when there are two strikes in the count. Another benefit of live batting practice is that hitters get practice at seeing the pitcher's release. Concentrating and being able to pick up the ball early in the pitcher's release is another key to becoming a good hitter.

### Scrimmage Games

If your coach will set up game situations at practice, this is the best practice of all for batters because everyone learns from pitchers working to batters in a game setting. You will learn how well your hitting skills have progressed as you face your team's pitching staff. You should also pick up on areas where you need improvement and discover things to concentrate on in future drills and practice.

## ADVANCED BATTING DRILLS

Next are some advanced batting drills, which are described as advanced because they are the most difficult drills in this book.

### Drop Drill

This drill can be dangerous, so make sure to set up and conduct it carefully under safe conditions. It starts like soft toss, with the batter set up to hit into a fence. The person who will drop the ball should be positioned slightly ahead of the batter's front foot, *and the dropper must be outside of the batter's swing arc.* The dropper holds the ball above shoulder level, says "trigger," and drops the ball through the batter's contact area. The batter strides when the dropper says "trigger," swings, and hits the ball as it drops. The main value of this drill is the development of a quick swing, bat speed, and making the batter focus on seeing and hitting the ball. It helps develop hand-eye coordination similar to other drills.

Drop drill

### Backdoor Toss Drill

This may be the most difficult drill of all. It sets up like the drop drill, but both the batter and tosser are facing the fence. The tosser should be three or four steps

Back door toss drill

behind the batter, who should be in the stance, looking back toward the tosser. The tosser says "trigger" and tosses the ball softly through the batter's strike zone. The batter strides with the "trigger" signal and swings to hit the ball as it passes through the strike zone. It requires a quick swing, good timing, and coordination to hit even the softest toss at the normal contact point.

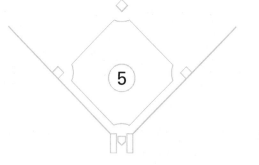

# GETTING READY TO BAT

The teammate ahead of you in the batting order has made an out, and it's your turn. Are you ready to bat? Of course, you say, you're always ready and eager to go to the plate. You've had pregame batting practice, you're loose, and your swing feels good. But are you really ready? The following are some things you can do in the dugout or the on-deck circle to help you have a good trip to the plate. You can look for keys that may give you an edge and up your odds of success against the pitcher. Being mentally prepared can eliminate some surprises when the pitches start flying.

## KNOW THE GAME SITUATION

"Having your head in the game" simply means that you are aware of the game situation at all times. You know the inning, the score, how many outs, and where runners, if any, are on base. Look for signals and be ready to do what the coach calls for. With a runner on base, you may get a bunt sign, hit-and-run sign, or the coach may try a steal with a fast runner. You can execute any of these things or you can hit away with confidence.

## YOUR ON-DECK JOB

When you are the on-deck batter, you have a responsibility when a runner is on base and may try to score on a play. Your job is to tell the runner whether to slide at home. When you anticipate a play at the plate, position yourself in back of the plate where the runner is coming down the baseline directly at you. Stand far enough away from the plate so you won't interfere with the play. If the play isn't going to be close, hold both hands high above your head and yell "stay up," directing the runner to score standing up. On a close play, push your hands palm down below your waist and yell "get down," meaning the runner should slide.

## STUDY THE PITCHER

Opposing pitchers warm up before the game, usually in plain sight of the other team. And it is amazing how little attention a team pays to the other pitcher's warm-up pitches. Pregame is a good time to size up a pitcher because during the warm-up you will likely see her total pitch assortment and get a feel of how well she can control her pitches. The reason teams don't observe other pitchers may be because players are busy with infield routines or other warm-up activities. If you don't have time to observe the warm-up, then the next option is to study the opposing pitcher from the dugout or the on-deck circle during the game.

When you do get a chance to watch, study her motion and how she releases the ball. See if she has a smooth delivery or if it is erratic and herky-jerky. Does she hide the ball well before the delivery or can you pick it up before the release? Try to pick up on how fast she is throwing her fastball. Notice if she has been blowing pitches past other batters on your team. Ask teammates what pitches they saw and how fast they were. If the pitcher is really fast, you may need to choke up on your bat a little to quicken your swing. Find out if her assortment of pitches includes a changeup or breaking pitches. Look for any pattern in how she uses certain pitches. She may always throw a changeup in certain situations. When you see such a pattern in her pitches, be ready to make her pay for getting into a rut with her pitch selection.

## WATCH THE COUNT

Watch how deep into the count the pitcher is going with other batters on your team. The pitcher is struggling with a control problem when she is walking batters or continually going deep into the count to 3–0, 3–1, or 3–2. In this case you may be very selective in the pitch you want to hit. You should not lose your aggressiveness at the plate; just don't help her by chasing bad pitches. Also take a walk if it comes but only when you don't get a decent pitch to hit.

Some pitchers throw an easy duck when they get behind in the count, and there is a good rationale for this. A pitcher knows there is no defense for a base on balls, so she may let up and throw a fat pitch just to get the ball across the plate. When you see this pattern, be ready to drive the pitch somewhere. Another good rationale is that pitchers want to get ahead in the count. Some of them want it badly enough to serve up a fat first pitch to each batter. When you see this pattern, take that first pitch deep.

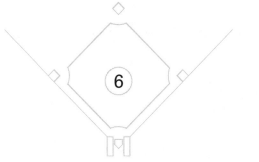

# MAKING YOUR AT BAT COUNT

Now you're in your stance at the plate, ready to face the pitcher in a game. Each time you go to the plate, you have an opportunity to make a contribution to your team's success. Most but not all of the time your objective is to get on base. When you aren't necessarily expected to reach base safely, the coach may want you to lay down a sacrifice bunt. In these situations the coach is expecting you to advance a runner on base, but we will cover bunting and bunt strategies later. For now, your objective is to hit away, try to reach base safely, and eventually score.

The pitcher has a natural statistical advantage. The best hitters in your league likely won't have a batting average above .400. This means they fail to get a hit six out of ten times. However, you can offset part of that advantage by being a smart hitter, and that's what this chapter is about.

## TWO REQUIREMENTS

Two major physical requirements are necessary to become a good hitter. Other nonphysical characteristics of good hitters, such as attitude, will be dealt with in a later chapter. The first physical requirement is solid swing mechanics, which must be smooth, consistent, and powerful. The second requirement is knowing the strike zone and knowing it well. The strike zone is defined as the area between your armpits and the top of your knees when you are in your normal batting stance, and it is also the width of home plate. Although you understand where the strike zone is, judging when a pitch is in this area while you are at bat is not so easy.

### The Window

This concept may help you get a good handle on the strike zone: think of it as a window in front of you as you are in your batting stance. It is as wide as the plate and extends from your armpits to the top of your knees.

Now, you will be looking for pitches to hit that will be passing through the window, and you will lay off those pitches outside of the window.

### Don't Bite on Bad Pitches

Striking out doesn't help your team at all, and many of the strikeouts at all age groups and skill levels are the result of swinging at bad pitches. The early age groups have a combination of aggressive batters and pitchers with not-so-good control. You must be aggressive at the plate, yet disciplined at the same time. While pitches in the middle of the strike zone are no problem to judge, watch out for low pitches. The tough ones are at the knees on the corners of the plate, and they are among the most difficult to hit well. Many batters go after pitches way below their knees.

Many players just can't lay off a high pitch, and few can hit it well enough to make swinging worthwhile. A pitch up near the eyes looks so big and inviting that it's hard to resist giving it a try. You may learn to let these high pitches go by thinking about the position of your hands. In your stance, your hands are at your armpits. Lay off any pitch above your hands.

## BE A CONTACT HITTER

The best way to help your team with your bat is to put the ball in play. You know the strike zone and have good swing mechanics, so concentrate on making solid contact with good pitches. When you make solid contact, the result will usually be a line drive, which is the best of all. However, when you put the ball in play, you force the other team to make a play to get an out, and putting pressure on a defense is always good. Some of your hits will be base hits, and others will force the defense to make errors. Even when the other team gets you out, you may advance a runner. Contact hitting can make many good things happen.

## WORK THE COUNT

Always know the ball and strike count. In an early age group most pitchers have only two pitches, a fastball and a changeup. Many of them will always try to throw a strike on the first pitch to get ahead of the batters. Be ready for that first pitch and drive it somewhere if it's a good one. Treat pitches the same way on any count with fewer than two strikes and three balls. If it's a good pitch, rip it.

If the count goes to 2–0, 3–0, or 3–1, you have the advantage. The coach may have you take a pitch on a 3–0 count, which is called a hitter's count. In each case you may be selective about the pitch you hit. The pitcher must throw strikes on these counts to avoid going deeper into the count or giving up a walk. If you don't like the pitch, let it go; you'll see another strike to hit or eventually draw a walk.

### Hitting with Two Strikes

When there are two strikes on you, you must make some adjustments. Now is the time to protect the plate and put the ball in play. Move forward in the batter's box, which will give you a better angle to hit the ball into fair territory. Also, choke up a little on your bat to give you better bat control and make your swing a little quicker. You don't want to take a called third strike. Be aggressive. If a pitch looks close to the strike zone, swing at it. Pitches can be "too close to take" with two strikes, and umpires are not always reliable.

Most young pitchers don't have much in the way of breaking pitches. But if the pitcher you're facing has a breaking pitch, you'll likely see it when the count is 0–2, 1–2, or 2–2. Don't guess. Always look for the fastball and adjust to a breaking pitch or off-speed pitch if necessary. If you're expecting an off-speed pitch or breaking ball, the pitcher may blow a fastball by you for the third strike.

## RELAX

During your career you will step to the plate in some really exciting, pressure-packed game situations. It is natural for you to be a bit nervous when the chips are down, the game is on the line, and you're at bat. Being a little worked up means you really care about the game's outcome. A little nervousness is healthy; however, heavy stress and tension can be debilitating to you as a batter.

Everyone reacts to pressure in different ways. Some players look forward to it, calmly bear down, and give it their best. In other players tension builds and muscles tighten to the point where making a good swing with the bat is almost impossible.

If you start to feel tension building up in your body, you must deal with it. First, call for a time-out and step out of the batter's box. Take a deep breath; then take an easy swing with your bat. Take time to calm yourself by looking at your coach as if you were getting a signal. Take another deep breath. You should start to feel the tension leaving your muscles. Now you're ready—step back into the box and whack the next good pitch.

**THE LONG BALL**

Smart hitters don't try to hit home runs. Most batters who try to hit homers on purpose lunge rather than stride. They swing off balance, overswing, or swing upward trying to lift the ball. And as a result of all this, they hit very few long balls and strike out a lot. Seeing every pitch as an opportunity to launch a ball out of the park is not smart hitting. Smart hitters stay with their solid mechanics; make a smooth, powerful swing; and concentrate on making solid contact. Smart hitters hit a lot of line drives, seldom strike out, carry a better batting average, and regularly contribute to team success. And once in a while, one of those line drives actually clears the outfield fence.

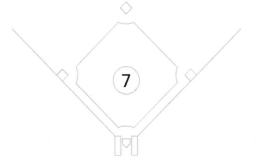

# BUNTING FUNDAMENTALS

It's fun to hit away. Nothing looks better to a hitter than a solid line drive going into a gap in the outfield. However, to become a total offensive player, you must learn to bunt. Bunting is a basic fundamental skill that all batters should develop, because the bunt can be a powerful offensive weapon. Good hand-eye coordination is needed for hitting, and the same goes for bunting. It's not as easy as it looks, and becoming a good bunter will take a lot of practice.

In the following section we describe a sacrifice bunt and two different bunting techniques: squaring around and contact position. Try each to see which technique works best for you. Then we will talk about the fake bunt, the drag bunt, and a hitting technique called "slap hitting." *Take care when attempting a bunt or slap hit.* If you make contact with the ball and either foot is outside the batter's box or is touching the plate, you can be automatically called out.

## SACRIFICE BUNT

This is the most basic bunt whose main purpose is to advance runners (as described in chapter 8). The mechanics of a sacrifice bunt are the same for left-handed and right-handed batters and for either bunting technique. Position yourself near the front of the batter's box. Don't make the movement obvious, as it may give away your intention. Moving to the front of the box gives you a better angle to reliably get the bunt down in fair territory as shown in the photo.

## SQUARE AROUND

When the pitcher is in the windup, square around to bunt. This means you turn your body and both feet so you are facing the pitcher. Your knees should be bent slightly for good balance. Grasp the bat near the knob with your bottom hand. Next slide your top hand about

Square around facing the pitcher

halfway up the barrel of the bat, holding it between your thumb and your bent index finger.

Be sure to keep your thumb and fingers behind the bat to prevent the pitched ball from injuring them.

Keep thumb and fingers behind the bat

Position the bat level to the ground in front of your body at about chest height and wait for the pitch. Practice the squaring around move so you can do it quickly. You want the bunt you lay down to surprise the defense.

## CONTACT POSITION

Another optional bunting technique is to take your normal batting stance in the front of the box. As the pitcher starts to release the pitch, quickly pivot on your back foot and turn with your stomach facing the pitcher. This is the basic contact position you learned in the chapter on batting fundamentals. Slide your top

Contact position

hand up the bat, holding it the same as in the squared-around bunting method. Hold the bat level at chest height as the pitch arrives.

You start with the bat at chest level in both techniques because in the worst case you want the bat movement to be downward toward the pitch. This increases your chances of getting the bunt on the ground. If you start with the bat lower and have to move it up to make contact, it increases the chances that you'll pop up the bunt.

As the pitch comes in, move your bat (keeping it level) into position to contact the ball. Don't move the bat forward toward the ball or peck at it. This punching movement can result in a weak ground ball in the infield. You want to make a fielder move toward the plate to field a bunt, rather than bunting the ball directly to her. Let the ball hit the bat as you hold it. When the pitch solidly strikes the bat, the ball will jump out and quickly die after rolling a short distance on the ground. This sacrifice bunt will force the defense to make a play.

## BUNTING PRACTICE DRILLS

### *The Glove Drill*

This drill should help you get used to making contact. If you are right-handed, either borrow a left-hander's

Glove drill

glove or put your glove on your right hand. Lefties either borrow a righty's glove or put their own glove on their left hand. Stand at the plate in your bunt position. Have someone throw medium-speed pitches over the plate. Reach out and let the ball hit the glove. You are not catching the ball, just using the glove to stop it. If you can get the glove in front of the pitch, you will be able to make contact when you bunt.

### The Placement Drill

The best sacrifice bunts will be down or near a baseline, not back at the pitcher. Use your hand near the knob of

Toward the third baseline

Toward the first baseline

the bat to angle the bat, making the bunt go toward either the first or third baseline. Lay out a string or something else to represent baselines. Have someone toss the ball to you, and practice letting the ball hit the bat, sending it down along a line. When you take batting practice with your team, always lay down a few bunts before you start to swing away.

## THE FAKE BUNT

The fake bunt is primarily a strategy move as you will learn in the next chapter. When you execute the fake bunt, you are really taking the pitch, but you want to learn something about the other team's bunt defense. To fake a bunt, square around exactly as you would for a sacrifice bunt. As the pitch comes in, jerk the bat back out of the strike zone. Umpires are not entirely trustworthy. If you leave the bat near the strike zone, even a bad pitch may be called a strike because the ump thought you offered at it.

The primary value of a fake bunt is to force the defense to reveal its bunt coverage. The catcher will usually be assigned to handle bunts within three or four steps out in front of the plate. Other than that, teams may have all different types of bunt coverage involving the first baseman, third baseman, and pitcher. If there is no reaction by the first or third basemen, the pitcher is the likely fielder on all bunts the catcher doesn't handle. Knowing how they intend to cover bunts will be to your team's advantage during later at bats.

## THE DRAG BUNT

While the sacrifice bunt is used to advance runners, the drag bunt is used to try to get a base hit. If you have fairly good speed, you should try to learn to drag bunt; however, drag bunting is not for every player. It takes very good timing, hand-eye coordination, and bat control.

For the right-handed batter, start again in the front of the batter's box to get the angle on fair territory. Your left foot should be close to the outside line of the batter's box. As the pitcher starts the delivery, quickly pivot into a sprinter's starting stance by stepping toward first base with your right foot. Bring the bat over the plate, holding it parallel to the ground and gripping it the same as for the sacrifice bunt. When the pitch comes in, let it hit the bat, sending it into fair territory.

The left-handed batter has an advantage when drag bunting because the lefty is two steps closer to first base than the right-handed batter. As the pitch is released, pivot into the sprinter stance by stepping toward first with the right foot. Hold the bat the same as when making a sacrifice bunt and angle it so you are aiming to place the ball toward the right side of the infield. You will actually be moving toward first base when the pitch arrives at the plate. Drag bunting is a good offensive tool if you can pull it off.

## SLAP HITTING

Slap hitting, like drag bunting, isn't for all players. Even if she normally bats right-handed, the slap hitter will move to the left-handed batter's box, which is closest to first base. She must have excellent timing, good hand-eye coordination, good bat control, and sprinter speed. The slap hitter starts in her stance in the back of the batter's box. She must get a running start because it is

Stance

Crossover step

Slap contact

critical that she surprise the defense. When the pitch is released, she takes a running start toward first base and flicks her bat out to slap the ball into the infield. Most slap hitters attempt to punch the ball toward the third base side of the infield. It is difficult to successfully execute a slap hit. The batter's timing must be almost perfect, and the pitch must be in a location where she can make good contact.

A good slap hitter has several advantages. A fast runner can use her speed to get on base, and she puts pressure on a defense. Infielders know that good contact by a batter with sprinter speed makes for tough plays, especially when the batter has a running start toward first base. If the defense pulls in, the shot she hits can be hard to handle, or the ball may be punched through the infield. Give slap hitting a try. With lots of practice you may be able to do it well.

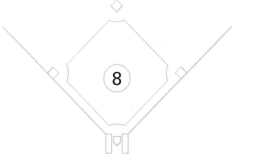

# ADVANCING BASE RUNNERS

To win games, you must score, but first you need runners on base. That's what batting and being a smart batter are all about. Teams with a strong offense know how
to execute plays that advance runners into scoring position. In the early age group league play, a runner on
second base with fewer than two outs will score a high
percent of the time. The following are proven methods
to advance runners.

## BUNTING

### *The Fake Bunt*

The fake bunt is a maneuver to make a defense reveal its bunt coverage. Your coach should have a signal for the fake bunt and wants to see what happens when you do it. Square around as the pitcher winds up, and draw your bat back out of the strike zone well before the ball arrives at the plate. The pitch may be a strike, but you can risk getting behind in the count in return for what you learn.

Pay attention to which infielders charge in toward the plate when you do the fake. In their bunt coverage, either or both the third and first basemen will charge in to make a play. Knowing who moves will come into use later in the right situation.

A fake bunt can accomplish other things. It can be a threat to teams that aren't very good at covering bunts. If it makes the team think, that's good. The first and third basemen may move in, making it easier to drive a ball past one of them. Some pitchers sling a wild pitch when they see a batter square, and a catcher may miss a pitch completely when she's distracted by a batter in a bunt stance.

### The Sacrifice Bunt

The sacrifice bunt is the best way to advance runners. With a runner on first base or runners on first or second base with fewer than two outs, your coach may signal for a sacrifice bunt. When asking for the sacrifice, the coach is willing to give up an out to advance runners into a better scoring position.

Square around as the pitcher starts her delivery using one of the bunt techniques you learned in chapter 7. Make sure you get the bunt down. A pop-up in this situation can result in an easy rally-killing double play. At least, the well-executed sacrifice should result in advanced runners and an out at first. And, sacrifice bunts don't count against your batting average.

There are other good possibilities on a sacrifice bunt play. A team always helps itself when pressure is exerted on the defense to make a play. A bunt could be misplayed, or a fielder may make a bad throw. Runs can be scored on a botched bunt play, or the bunt could be so good that you beat the throw to first.

### The Squeeze Play

A squeeze is used when there is a runner on third and fewer than two outs. The squeeze play is not a high-percentage play in fast-pitch softball because the runners cannot lead off base prior to the pitch. If a coach tries a squeeze play, it is a surprise tactic that attempts to trade an out for a run. The batter must wait until the pitcher has almost released the pitch, then square to bunt. On a suicide squeeze, the runner breaks toward home as the pitch is released. The batter must get the bunt down, and the runner must be fast and get a good break off the base.

Another way to score on a squeeze play is a delayed squeeze, also called a safety squeeze. In this, the runner moves off the base and tries to score when the play is made on the runner at first. This also requires a fast runner and good timing to beat a throw from first to home.

### Beating Bunt Defenses

When you or a player on your team does a fake bunt, the infield should reveal its bunt defense. The variations in defenses involve the first and third basemen and the pitcher. The catcher will usually take any bunts within two or three steps of the plate. If either the first baseman or third baseman charges in and the other stays in position, bunt down the line away from the one who charges. If neither one charges, this means the pitcher will handle all bunts. In this case bunt down either baseline. If all three charge, try to bunt to either side of the pitcher, between the charging players. If two of them go after the ball, you may create a mix-up.

A fake bunt or sacrifice bunt can reveal a defense that is weak on bunt coverage. When this happens, a coach may call for several bunts in a row until the defense proves it can make the plays. These simple dribblers in the infield can thus become a powerful offensive weapon.

## THE BATTER'S ROLE IN STEALING BASES

Stealing bases is a direct attempt to advance runners. The batter must get the steal signal and react as follows in each situation:

◆ *Straight steal*—The runner will break with the release of the pitch. The batter strides and acts as if she will swing but takes the pitch. Or at the coach's direction, with fewer than two strikes, the batter may swing at the pitch to try to protect the runner.

◆ *Hit-and-run*—In a hit-and-run play the runner breaks with the pitch, and the batter is expected to put the ball in play. Good contact hitters are valuable in hit-and-run plays. However, in a hit-and-run, the batter swings at the pitch no matter where it is located. This is like a straight steal with the batter hitting away.

◆ *Fake bunt and steal*—If the third baseman charges in on a fake bunt or a real bunt when there is a runner on second, this presents a real opportunity. In this bunt coverage, the shortstop will cover third base. It works like this: The runner breaks toward third with the pitch. The batter fake bunts, pulling the third baseman in. A footrace begins between the runner and the shortstop who is trying to cover third base. A runner with average speed should win this race to the bag 80 or 90 percent of the time. This play can score a run if the shortstop doesn't handle the throw at third.

♦ *Delayed steal*—This maneuver requires the base runner to have much better than average speed. Watch how the catcher returns the ball to the pitcher. If she starts to get lazy, lobbing her return throw to the pitcher, you may be able to steal a base. Take a walking lead off base and break toward the next base as the catcher releases her throw. To pull this off successfully requires good timing, good foot speed, and the ability to make a good slide at the base. Usually this is a close play.

**SUMMARY**

To carry out the plays in this chapter, a team must be fundamentally sound. A team with a good offense can execute these plays when the situation warrants. All that is required is:

1. Average or above-average foot speed
2. Players who can reliably get a bunt into play
3. Batters who can make contact when needed
4. Base runners who can make good slides

All of the plays in this chapter put pressure on a defense to make a play. And, defenses don't always get it right. Sometimes a simple attempt to move a runner can result in game-winning runs.

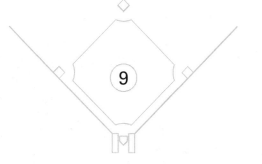

# RUNNING THE BASES

At most your team will only get twenty-one outs in a regulation game. Each runner who reaches base represents an opportunity to score. Smart baserunning can win ball games, and bad baserunning usually results in outs that can cause losses. Speed on the bases is wonderful, but it cannot make up for bad baserunning. In this chapter we will describe situations and how a base runner should react. In most cases a base coach will be directing you with voice and/or hand signals. However, this does not absolve you from the responsibility of also having your head in the game and being a smart, skilled base runner.

## RUN THROUGH FIRST BASE

You have hit a ground ball to the infield and are running toward first base. This may sound dumb, but you must run all the way to the base. One of the things that can make a coach crazy is a runner who hesitates as she reaches the base. In younger leagues a lot of runners are thrown out when they slow down as they reach first base. Another bad mistake is when a runner makes a leap toward the base. Many times these runners are in the air when the throw arrives.

The quickest way to first base is to run as hard as you can and run through the base. Don't slow down until *after* you've crossed the base. After you cross the base, veer to the right into foul territory. If you turn to the left into fair territory, you may be judged to be offering to advance toward second base and can be tagged out. However, if the play is botched at first and your coach says for you to go, head for second as fast as possible. When you cross the foul line back into fair territory, you must then reach second base or return to first before being tagged out.

### Round the Bases

You have hit the ball into the outfield. If the hit is to right field, run through first base the same as if you've hit an infield ground ball. On a hard-hit ball, many runners are thrown out at first by an alert right fielder. If you've hit the ball toward left or center field, run toward first and veer slightly toward foul territory as you approach the base. This direction allows you to round first base and get on the quickest course toward second. Touch the inside edge of the base with your right foot and round the base as if you were going to advance to second. If it's a base hit and your coach tells you to hold up, take the turn toward second base and return to first. If the ball is caught by a fielder, pull up and go to the dugout. Listen to your coach. The ball may get past a fielder. If the coach tells you to go, run to second as fast as you can. As you near second base, look at your third base coach. The coach should be signaling you to slide, hold, or continue to third. Again as you near third base, the coach may send you home or hold you up. If the coach says to slide, get down without question. As you near home, the on-deck batter should be in position to tell you whether to slide or score standing up.

As you run the bases on an extra-base hit, run so that you can round the base as you approach each one. Rounding lets you run straight in the base path to the next base. The fastest path when you are going from first around second base to third or from second around third to home will be rounding each base, touching each on the inside corner with your right foot.

## BE SMART

The following describes several situations in which you are a base runner, and in the final section, situations when you must always run. But when tagging up, stealing, and in other instances, it is not mandatory that you run. If you stumble or get a bad break off the base, pull up and go back to the base. Another opportunity will come. It is far better to be smart and not try to force a play after a bad start than to run into a sure out.

### On Base

When you're on base, keep your head in the game. Know the ball and strike count and the number of outs. Coaches shouldn't need to control every move by a base runner. Outs, the count, and some other circumstances can trigger automatic responses by base runners. If you're not sure about the count or number of outs, ask your coach or the base umpire.

You can't lead off base before the pitch leaves the pitcher's hand. But you can be ready to advance if needed. Before each pitch, get into a sprinter's stance with your front foot ready to push off against the base. When the pitch is released, take a couple of quick running steps toward the next base. This can give you a moving start in case you need to run.

*Don't take your eyes off the ball.* Be ready to run on each pitch. Watch for a wild pitch or passed ball, as either should result in a free base. Don't lead off base so far that the catcher can pick you off. The coach should warn you to get back if the catcher throws. If there is no opportunity to run on a pitch, immediately return to the base.

If a batted ball touches you in fair territory and you are not on a base, you will automatically be called out. When you are the runner at third, take your leadoff

Sprinter stance

steps in foul territory, because if a teammate rips a foul down the line and it touches you, it is only a foul ball.

### Tagging Up

You are the runner on third base, and there are fewer than two outs. The batter hits a fly ball to the outfield. Your third base coach tells you to tag up. Go to the base and set up in a sprinter's stance facing home plate. When the outfielder catches the ball, the coach should tell you to go. Break hard for the plate as soon as you hear "go." When you are at least halfway to the plate, look for the on-deck batter telling you to slide or stand up.

If the fly ball is not hit in the field deep enough (in the coach's judgement) for you to score, the coach may have you tag up and fake going toward home to draw a throw. If so, take three or four running steps toward home after the catch, stop, and return toward third. If you sell the act well enough, you may draw a bad throw and score after all.

You are the runner at second base, again with fewer than two outs. The batter hits a fly ball to deep right field. The base coach may tell you to tag up and advance to third after the catch. This can happen on a deep fly ball or when the coach has noticed that the fielder doesn't have a strong arm. Again, go to the base, set up in the sprinter's stance, and advance to third on "go." Watch for the coach's slide or stand-up signal as you approach third. Tagging up at first to advance to second is a low percentage play because second base is too close to all outfield positions.

### Go Halfway

In each of the following halfway cases, the ball must be hit deep into the outfield. The purpose of these maneuvers is to give you a head start if the fielder can't make the catch.

You are on first base, and there are fewer than two outs. A fly ball is hit to right field. Go a little less than halfway to second and return to the base immediately if the ball is caught.

Go halfway on a ball hit to left or center field, and, again, return when the ball is caught. If the fielder misses the ball, you have a head start to the next base.

You are on second base with fewer than two outs. A fly ball is hit to the outfield, and the coach has not told you to tag up. Go part of the way toward third and return to second if the ball is caught. If the ball is misplayed, you may score.

In all of these situations, you should not go so far off base that you can be doubled off after a catch.

### Stealing Bases

The coach will decide when to put on the steal signal. You can't lead off, so get in your sprinter's stance. If you are fast, you may be able to steal both second and third on a catcher with a weak arm. Take off toward the base at the pitch release and be prepared to slide when you reach it.

A good time to steal second is when there are runners on first and third with fewer than two outs. Often teams will concede the steal rather than risk giving up a run by making a play at second. Both the coach and the runner at third must be alert. Some teams automatically try to pick off the runner at third base as the other runner steals second. Other teams throw quickly to the pitcher who then tries to pick the runner off third. Then there are teams that concede nothing and go after the runner stealing second. It is up to the coach's judgment whether to send a runner home when the play is at second.

### Always Run

You will always run when you are on any base, there are two outs, and the batter hits the ball.

You will always run when there are two outs, a 3–2 count on the batter, and (1) when you are on first base,

(2) when you are on second base and a runner is on first, or (3) when you are on third and both first and second bases are occupied.

You will always run when a ground ball is hit in the infield and you may be forced at the next base. Be careful—when you are on first base with less than two outs and the batter hits an infield ground ball you must run to second. When the infielder takes the throw at second for the force—slide, no matter how far you are from second base. The relay throw to complete the double play can be close to your head. Getting down by sliding can prevent a potentially serious injury.

You will usually run when a wild pitch or passed ball goes to the backstop. When you are on third base, attempt to score only if the coach sends you.

### SLIDE!

Good base runners are also good at sliding into the bases. A player who knows how to slide can somtimes avoid a tag when other players would be easily put out. Sliding is potentially dangerous, so practicing to develop the skill could also be regarded as injury prevention. You should learn the slide techniques that are feetfirst toward a base. *Do not slide headfirst.* Colliding with the base or a fielder can cause a serious injury.

Straight-in slide

Hook slide to right

Wear sliding pads in both games and practice. To practice, find a place with sand or loose dirt to minimize a potential injury. Measure off about a sixty-foot distance to your sliding spot and set up something flat to serve as a base. You don't want to jam a foot or knee in practice. Run at full speed toward the base to practice a straight-in slide and hook slides to both the right and left side of the base.

At first it will be hard to judge how far from the base to start your slide. With practice you will learn to just make it to the base without coming up short or oversliding. When you slide, keep your feet and legs close to the ground to practice sliding under a high tag.

# A POSITIVE APPROACH
# TO HITTING

Throughout this book we have stressed the mechanics necessary to be a good hitter and complete offensive player. You have learned how to set up, make a good swing, run the bases, bunt, and advance runners. You know how to make a contribution to your team's success. The final thing that can help you become a very good hitter is what goes on between your ears. Granted, it may be easy to have negative thoughts in an activity where you know it's likely you won't succeed 60 or 70 percent of the time. The critical difference that will make you a very good hitter is your attitude.

## STAY POSITIVE

There is an old saying that can't never did. If you go to the plate with the thought that you can't hit the pitcher you're facing, you might as well leave your bat in the dugout. Your attitude must remain positive at all times. Sure, the pitcher looks fast, but you will figure out a way to hit. Maybe you'll shorten up on the bat and get around on the fastball. Or perhaps you'll crowd the plate to try to take it away from her. No pitcher is unbeatable. You know your abilities, you can put the ball in play. Trust your swing. If she gets you this time, you'll hit her the next time up.

## BE CONFIDENT

Good hitters are confident. They believe they can make good, solid contact on almost any pitch in the strike zone. Once they have watched a pitcher work and looked at a couple of pitches, they believe they have an edge. Good hitters know the strike zone, and they know the pitcher's job is to throw strikes. Although a batter can be fooled on a pitch, a good hitter knows it only takes one pitch and when it comes she will put it into play.

There is a thin line between being confident and being cocky, and a high level of success at the plate can lead to a cocky attitude. As soon as a player starts to think and behave like she invented the game, a fall is likely. Have confidence in your abilities, focus on the game, and keep your successes and failures in perspective. In the long run, you will earn what you get from the game.

## BE AGGRESSIVE

Good hitters are aggressive. They don't passively stand and take pitches looking for a walk. They are always looking for a good pitch, ready to drive it somewhere. This is not all-out "swing-at-anything" aggressiveness, but controlled aggression. It takes a knowledge of the strike zone and discipline to lay off bad pitches. Good hitters seldom take a called third strike and seldom strike out on bad pitches.

## DEAL WITH PRESSURE

A good hitter can perform under pressure and enjoys the challenge of being at bat when the game is on the line. To be a little nervous is normal in a pressure situation. But the good hitter knows when the stress of a situation starts to make her tense. She knows that tense muscles can't perform well, and she relieves her tension by stepping out of the batter's box to take a couple of deep breaths. She takes a look at the coach as if looking for a signal and makes a couple of practice swings to loosen her muscles. She steps back into the box ready to do her best, knowing that the pitcher is also subject to the pressure of the situation.

In this pressure situation, guard against making changes. You must concentrate on each pitch, stay with your sound mechanics, and trust your swing. Think contact first. You must at least put the ball into play, which will shift pressure to the defense to make a play. Think positive: Maybe you'll hit a shot into an outfield gap and clear the bases. Perhaps your hit will force a defensive error, or the pitcher will give in to the pressure and walk you. In any of these possibilities, your team gains.

## DEALING WITH A SLUMP

Unfortunately, at times batters go through a period when they can't buy a hit. It happens to all batters and is called a slump. Play long enough and it will also happen to you. The problem with a slump is that it not only gets into your batting average, but it can also get into your head. One of the responses to a slump is for batters to try harder, and this can lead to an aggressiveness that can be self-defeating. So, how do you deal with a slump?

You must be positive. It may take some time, but tell yourself that you'll work it out. Think about what is happening. If you're not making good contact and are striking out a lot, something has changed in your mechanics. Go back to the basic drills on mechanics and practice, practice, practice. Perhaps you're moving your head, overswinging, or taking your eye off of the ball. Don't let a slump get you down on yourself. Chapter 12 of this book may help you find the problem.

However, when you are in a slump but are making good contact, take heart. It may seem for a while that every shot you hit is right at a fielder. There is such a thing as hitter's luck, and it can be either good or bad. You may just be going through a bad run of luck. If you're making good contact with the ball, stay positive and keep making your good swing. Things have a way of evening out. For every time you go through the frustration of hitting balls at fielders, you will likely go through another period when getting hits seems to be easy. Your line drives are out of the reach of fielders, and even weak ground balls seem to have "seeing eyes" as they find holes and go through the infield.

## BELIEVE IN YOURSELF

You have worked hard to develop sound mechanics and a good swing. You have a positive can-do attitude.

From game experiences you know your strengths as a hitter. No one can expect you to give more than your best, so give your best effort with each at bat and accept the outcome, either good or not so good. Above all, stay positive and keep your head up.

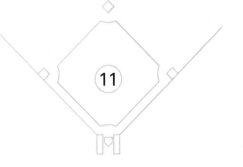

# TEAM OFFENSE

Good offensive teams have fun. They also win more than their fair share of the games they play. When all players understand their roles and the strategies of the game, good things happen. To be successful, a team doesn't need to be loaded with superstars. A group of players pulling together and making individual contributions can go a long way.

These good offensive teams have many common characteristics, as outlined in the following:

◆ *Respect*—The team shows respect for each other, its coaches, the other team, fans, and umpires.

- *Listening to coaches*—The good teams listen to their coaches. Players don't miss signals, and they execute what the coach wants.

- *Good mechanics*—The batters have good mechanics and tight, compact swings. There aren't any wannabe home run hitters in the lineup.

- *Discipline*—The batters know the strike zone very well. They lay off bad pitches, which puts pressure on opposing pitchers to throw strikes. They work the count, knowing when to take a pitch and when to swing when a pitch is too close to take. Disciplined players seldom take a called third strike.

- *Aggressive at bat*—Batters are aggressive. They go to the plate to hit, not beg for walks. They make contact with pitches, putting the ball in play, which puts pressure on defenses to make plays.

- *Controlling the game tempo*—Players recognize when opposing pitchers are working too fast from pitch to pitch. They break the tempo by calling time-out, stepping out of the batter's box, looking for a signal, and taking a couple of swings. They use these delaying tactics to slow down a fast-working pitcher. They also gain time to get set for the next pitch.

◆ *Aggressiveness on the bases*—Base runners are aggressive, yet controlled. They are smart base runners who force teams to make plays.

◆ *Good bunters*—All players can be relied on to get a bunt down when it is needed. The swiftest runners can occasionally put down a drag bunt for a base hit.

◆ *Staying within limitations*—Players and coaches know individual characteristics. Players play within their limitations and each does her best. For example, a slow runner wouldn't be expected to steal bases, but she can be relied on to be a smart base runner.

◆ *Pulling together*—They know that rallies require the contribution of several players. Although there may be stars on the team, they know that no one player can generate enough offense to carry a team.

◆ *Positive attitude*—Good teams "can do." They believe in themselves and their teammates. No player lets up; each gives her best effort on each play.

- *Positive support*—Individuals support each other and offer help to others if needed. They recognize and compliment the contributions of others. They cheer for and encourage teammates at every chance.

- *Heads in the game*—The players understand game-winning strategies. They always know the game situation and are ready to implement whatever action the coach wants.

- *Offering no excuses*—Players do their best. They don't make excuses when things don't go as planned. The response is to bear down harder and get the job done the next time.

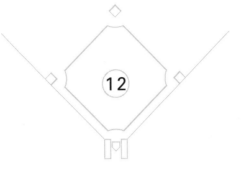

# COMMON BATTER PROBLEMS

Throughout this book we have concentrated on a positive approach to batting and offensive play. The emphasis has been on developing and maintaining sound hitting mechanics and keeping a positive, disciplined, aggressive mind-set. However, during the course of a season some hitters' effectiveness starts to tail off because of some change in either mechanics or the approach to hitting. Some of these changes are conscious; others occur without the player being aware of them.

Below, we describe several habits batters fall into that can limit their effectiveness. Any deviations from sound batting mechanics are usually easy to spot by a teammate, coach, or parent when a player's form is measured against the points in chapter 2, "Batting Fundamentals."

It is usually more difficult to diagnose changes in a player's mental approach to hitting because the player must recognize and solve the problem herself. In many cases, the root cause of changes in mechanics is a result of a change in a player's mind-set. We will start with such a possibility.

## THE HOME RUN COMPLEX

A home run is a wonderful sight as the ball soars over the outfield fence. A batter with sound mechanics and a good, compact swing will hit a long ball occasionally. But if a home run is not viewed in the proper perspective, it can lead to a batter's downfall. Much flap will be made of the homer by players, coaches, and fans. If the batter views the event as a good thing, takes it in stride, and maintains her disciplined approach to hitting, she will continue to be a good hitter.

But life in the spotlight is good, and the batter decides she can hit more home runs. Following are departures from sound batting mechanics that players make when trying to hit the long ball on purpose. These changes, which are fairly easy to spot, almost always lead to strikeouts. They can only be fixed after the player changes her objective and approach toward hitting.

♦ *Upswinging*—This is an attempt to lift the ball out of the park. When a batter abandons a tight, compact, level swing, strikeouts will multiply.

♦ *Overstriding or lunging*—With this the batter tries to get more body weight behind the bat, searching for power. Overshifting the body affects balance, which negates the firm, balanced foundation needed for consistent contact with the ball.

♦ *Overswinging*—Swing hard to hit hard, right? Well this is true up to the point where the swing throws the batter off balance. Then, batting consistency falls off. Again, good balance is a critical element in good hitting.

♦ *Foot in the bucket*—A batter who strides down the baseline, attempting to pull the ball is said to put her foot in the bucket. While a dead pull hitter may be able, on occasion, to drive an inside pitch, pitches down the middle or on the outside part of the plate will usually result in a ground ball to the infield *if* contact is made. To make consistent contact, the stride should be directly toward the pitcher.

+ *Heavier bat*—More lumber, more distance on contact, right? No, a bat that is too heavy will slow the swing and can also affect balance. Bat speed is an important part of both consistency and power.

A final thought about the home run complex: a batter with sound mechanics will usually hit line drives. But once in a while she will make solid contact and send the ball out of the park. It can and will happen without consciously trying to do it with each at bat.

**PROBLEMS WITH THE SETUP**

+ *Foot placement*—Setting up with the feet less than shoulder width apart can invite lunging with the stride and an off-balance swing. If the feet are too far apart in the setup, the batter is robbed of power, and may be off balance when striding.

+ *Hands too high*—High hands (above the shoulder) in the setup position affects the swing arc. To get to the proper ready position requires an adjustment of the hands as the pitcher starts the delivery, and this can result in a late swing.

+ *Bat not in the ready position*—The quickest path from the setup to the ball is with the bat at a forty-five degree angle to the ground. Batters who set up with the bat sticking straight up in the air or with the barrel drooping toward the ground waste motion getting to the contact point. This can also result in a late swing.

♦ *Setup too far from the plate*—Some batters set up so far from the plate that it is impossible to contact an outside pitch. In the stance make sure your bat arc covers the outside corners.

## OTHER PROBLEMS

♦ *Head movement*—Good hitters see the bat hit the ball. Having a steady head is a cornerstone of consistent hitting. Pulling the head takes the eyes off of the ball, making consistent contact almost impossible.

♦ *Too aggressive*—The most noticeable symptom of this problem is chasing bad pitches. First, get back to the basics. You must know the strike zone. The problem is solved as soon as the player develops the discipline to let bad pitches go. Being aggressive at the plate is good as long as there is some control.

♦ *Loopy swing*—This is the opposite of the tight, compact swing. Some batters think they can generate more power with arms fully extended throughout the swing. These swings generally have slower bat speed, affect the batter's balance, and make it hard to contact a pitch on the inside part of the plate. A fast pitcher usually blows a fastball past these batters.

The loopy swing may be a result of using a bat that is too heavy. Check for proper bat weight in chapter 2 in the section "Getting Started Right— Bat Selection."

◆ *Loss of confidence*—This is probably the worst thing that can happen to a batter. Good hitters have no room for negative thoughts. Even when things seem to be at their worst, good hitters believe they will drive the next pitch. Stay with sound mechanics, be aggressive, trust your swing, and believe in yourself. You can get the job done.

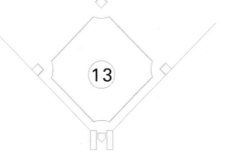

# FINAL THOUGHTS

In the past few years, the increase in participation of young women playing softball has been phenomenal. In many locales the number of softball participants equals the number of male counterparts playing youth league baseball. Starting at an early age in league play many of these young girls aspire to compete at higher levels on traveling teams, all-star teams, their high school teams, and eventually college teams.

That women's softball has arrived worldwide is reinforced by its accreditation as a full Olympic sport. Television coverage has brought the game into homes.

And there are now organized professional leagues so that players can extend their careers beyond college.

Successful young softball players love the game. They work hard at developing and improving their skills and have lots of fun playing. Playing the game well and having fun while doing it are worthwhile rewards. And for the really talented players, the opportunity for even greater rewards unfolds as they advance through the high school level to colleges and universities where softball players can earn scholarships.

The opportunity for a young woman to get a scholarship to play softball in college was rare a decade ago. But thanks to gender equity rules, there are many opportunities today. As competition intensifies at the college level, the demand for good players has increased. College coaches today scout high school games seeking skilled players at all positions. The door is open for the player who has the dedication and work ethic to excel at the game.

# ABOUT THE AUTHORS

Jacque Hunter, a veteran of twenty-nine years of coaching at New Albany High School in Indiana, was inducted into the Indiana High School Coaches Hall of Fame in 2003. During his coaching career, his teams have won eleven sectional titles, seven regional titles, made six appearances at the Indiana State Finals, were two times state runner-up, and won one Indiana State Championship. In 1996 he was the first coach in Indiana to record 300 victories and his teams notched number 400 in 2003. After the 2005 season his overall coaching record stood at 444 wins and 144 losses. Coach Hunter is a two-time State All-Star Team Coach and has received numerous Coach of the Year honors at the district, conference, and state levels. Coach Hunter is the coauthor of *A Guide for Young Softball Pitchers*.

Don Oster is a longtime baseball player and coach. His teams have won state championships at both Little League and Babe Ruth League levels. As a pitching coach, he had teams competing in four Babe Ruth League World Series. He is the author of *Largemouth Bass*, and coauthor of *A Guide for Young Pitchers*, *A Guide for Young Batters & Baserunners*, *A Young Player's Guide to Fielding and Defense*, *A Guide for Young Softball Pitchers*, *Hunting Today's Whitetail*, and *Pronghorn Hunting*. He resides in southern Indiana.

## DATE DUE